THE ILIAD

by
Homer

Teacher [illegible]

Written by
Gloria Levine, M. A.

Note
The text used to prepare this guide was the Anchor Books/Doubleday translation by Robert Fitzgerald. The page references may differ in other editions.

Please note: Please assess the appropriateness of this book for the age level and maturity of your students prior to reading and discussing it with your class.

ISBN 1-56137-752-X

Printed in the United States of America.

To order, contact your local school supply store, or—

Novel Units, Inc.
P.O. Box 791610
San Antonio, TX 78279

Web site: www.educyberstor.com

Table of Contents

Overview

The *Iliad* is considered one of the Western World's fountainheads of literature and culture. The *Iliad* and its sequel, the *Odyssey,* are the oldest epic poems in Western literature. Like the Bible, the *Iliad* is valued for both form and content—for its powerful language and its compelling story. The *Iliad* focuses on a few days toward the end of the ten-year Trojan War between the Greeks and the Trojans. (The *Odyssey* is about one soldier's homecoming, after the end of that war).

It is crucial for readers to remember that the *Iliad* was originally intended to be heard, not read. Whether or not Homer was a real man is up for debate—although most people believe that he was a real, possibly blind bard who lived around the 8th century B.C. We do know that the *Iliad* was originally recited orally—by Homer or by a legendary figure or group of people. We aren't sure when it was first written down. Not many people in Homer's time were literate, but it is possible that Homer may have written out the poem himself or had a scribe do it—or it may have been written down only after many years of oral transmission.

We do know that some of what is depicted in the *Iliad* and the *Odyssey* really happened. Archeologists have discovered that ancient Troy did exist (in modern-day Turkey) and that a Trojan War did take place, sometime in the early 1100s B.C. The *Iliad,* like Arthurian legend, purports to tell of a much earlier age, a few hundred years earlier—not the time period when Homer lived.

Homer took a lot of traditional material—developed by bards over many centuries—and cast it in a unique form. He used a great deal of repetition and formulaic phrasing—largely as a memory aid in the telling of this lengthy poem.

Students today—almost 2,000 years after Homer's time—can still find this story an exciting one that is relevant to their lives. This guide is intended to help you help them find common threads between their world (with its Power Rangers, global and ethnic conflicts, gender issues, etc.) and the one that Homer describes.

Plot Summary

Book One: Quarrel, Oath, and Promise

Homer invokes the Muse to "sing" the poem, beginning with the conflict between Agamémnon and Akhilleus. Akhilleus is outraged by Agamémnon's refusal to return a captive girl, Khryseis, to her father. Apollo has taken sides with the father and has punished the Greeks by killing many men in battle and visiting a plague on their camp. Akhilleus threatens to withdraw his support from Agamémnon—who has been fighting the Trojans ever since one of them (Paris) ran off with his brother Menelaos' wife (Helen)—and sail for home. An angry Agamémnon finally agrees to give Khryseis up—but takes lovely Brisêis from Akhilleus, in return. Akhilleus tells his mother Thetis (a goddess) the whole story and appeals to her to talk to Zeus and convince him to make Agamémnon pay by taking the Trojan side against the Greeks. This appeal causes discord on Olympus, as Zeus' wife Hêra sides with the Greeks. (Since Paris decided that Aphrodítê was even lovelier than Hêra, Aphrodítê rewarded Paris—a Trojan—by helping him obtain Menelaos' wife, Helen—a Greek—and so began the war between Greeks and Trojans.)

Book Two: Assembly and Muster of Armies

Acting on Thetis's request that Zeus help Akhilleus, Zeus sends Agamémnon a false dream which makes him think that Troy is about to fall. As a result, the Greeks are deceived into preparing for battle even though Akhilleus has already sailed off. Nestor (Greek) suggests that the army should be organized by nation and clan to foster loyalty. A long list of Greek commanders is given, followed by a shorter catalogue of Trojans.

Book Three: Dueling for a Haunted Lady

Paris (Trojan) agrees to face Menelaos (the Greek whose wife he snatched). Many of the Trojans want Helen to go back to her husband so that the war will end. Aphrodítê intervenes during the contest and sends Paris safely to his bedroom. The goddess of love also sends Helen, against Helen's will. Helen goes to bed with Paris, but reluctantly. The Greeks declare themselves victorious, since Paris has disappeared, and demand the return of Helen to Menelaos.

Book Four: A Bowshot Bringing War

Back on Olympus, the gods are having a big feast. Zeus irritates his wife, Hêra, (who sides with the Greeks) by saying that Troy should be spared and the war should end now, with Helen going back to Menelaos. Athêna disguises herself and tricks Pándaros (a Trojan archer) into shooting at Menelaos. Menelaos is only nicked, but the truce is broken and the war resumes with heavy casualties on both sides.

Book Five: A Hero Strives with Gods

The Greek warrior Diomêdês dominates the fighting, killing Pándaros. Several gods and goddesses get involved: Athêna and Hêra on the side of the Greeks; Apollo, Aphrodítê, and Arês on the side of the Trojans. Diomêdês wounds Aineías, but Apollo and Aphrodítê rescue him. Diomêdês also wounds Aphrodítê and Arês, who return to Olympus. There, Zeus sympathizes with Aphrodítê, but not with Arês—whom everyone hates. Neither side comes out ahead.

Book Six: Interludes in Field and City

The gods gone, the mortals continue to do battle. The Greeks pull ahead. On the urging of his brother, Hektor returns to Troy to instruct the women to make offerings to Athêna, so that she will rein in Diomêdês. Fierce Agamémnon vows to slaughter the Trojans, including women and children. Diomêdês and Glaukos are about to fight when they discover that their grandfathers have sworn friendship, so these two desist.

Book Seven: A Combat and a Rampart

Hektor has a duel with Aiax; neither side wins. A truce is called so that burials can be made. The Greeks build a rampart around their camp. The Trojans want Paris to give back Helen. He refuses, but agrees to give up the treasure that he had brought to Troy with Helen. The Greeks refuse the offer, however, and night falls.

Book Eight: The Battle Swayed by Zeus

Zeus gives the order that the gods—especially Hêra and Athêna—are not to join in the fight. Hektor leads the Trojans in driving the Greeks back to their encampment. Zeus predicts that Akhilleus will join the fray after his friend, Patroklos is killed—and until then, Hektor will keep the Greeks hopping, with no letup. Instead of going back to the city when it gets dark, the Trojans bivouac on the field and prepare to attack the next day.

Book Nine: A Visit of Emissaries

Diomêdês gives the demoralized Greeks a pep talk. That night, three Greeks—Phoenix, Odysseus, and Aías—approach Akhilleus and ask him to return to the battle, but he rejects their appeal.

Book Ten: Night in the Camp: A Foray

Old Nestor suggests that a reconnaisance patrol be done. Odysseus and Diomêdês go on a night expedition behind the Trojan lines. They capture Dolôn—a Trojan scout—and tricking him into thinking that his life will be spared, get information from him about the Trojans' battle plans. Then Diomêdês kills him. Next they kill the Thracian King Rhêsos and several of his men and take his lovely chariot horses.

Book Eleven: Prowess and Wounds of Akhaians

The Greeks are looking good at the beginning of their attack, but their heroes begin to get hurt, one after another. Diomêdês is wounded by Paris; Odysseus and Makháôn (a physician) are hurt, too. Zeus sends a message via Iris to Hektor: Stay out of the battle until Agamémnon is hurt. Agamémnon, who has been mercilessly killing Trojans right and left, is finally wounded himself, by Koôn; Hektor joins the fray. The Greeks draw back and Akhilleus begins to think about helping. He sends his good friend Patroklos to Nestor to ask about the wounded man Nestor is tending (Makháôn). Nestor reminds Patroklos that he is supposed to be counseling Akhilleus, and suggests that Patroklos advise Akhilleus to let Patroklos lead the Myrmidons into battle against the Trojans, wearing Akhilleus' armor. When Eurypylos (Greek) is wounded by Paris, Patroklos comes to the wounded man's aid.

Book Twelve: The Rampart Breached

The gods are still staying out of the battle, for the moment. Led by Hektor, the Trojans press on against the Greeks and reach the Greek fortifications. Poulydamas (Trojan) suggests that the Trojans would be better off going across the moat on foot; Hektor follows this advice, but rejects a second suggestion later based on a portent—that the army should retreat. Sarpêdôn leads an attack on the wall of the Greek fort. Hektor storms through the gates, and the Greeks flee to their ships.

Book Thirteen: Assault on the Ships

Zeus is confident that no gods will interfere on either side of the mortals' combat, but Poseidon mobilizes the Greeks. Vigor renewed, the Greeks make a stand around two fiery warriors, the two Aías. Hektor kills Amphimakhos, Poseidon's grandson, enraging the god, who protects Idómeneus (King of Krete) and Antilokohos as they fight fiercely against the Trojans. The Trojans push on, rallied by Hektor as they falter. Zeus plans to give the Trojans a limited victory without letting the Greeks be totally defeated.

Book Fourteen: Beguilement on Mount Ida

The Greeks are in terrible shape at first—with Diomêdês, Odysseus and Agamémnon all wounded. Odysseus condemns Agamémnon's plan to launch the ships as cowardly. Seeing that the Greeks are in desperate straits, Hêra is spurred into action. With the help of Aphrodítê and Sleep, Hêra seduces Zeus and puts him to sleep. Then she urges Poseidon to take advantage of the situation, and he doubles his efforts to help the Greeks. Hektor is wounded with a stone and carried off by his fellow Trojans, as they are driven back.

Book Fifteen: The Lord of Storm
Zeus revives, furious about Hêra's trickery. He sends Iris with a message to Poseidon, forcing him to withdraw; the Trojans push forward against the Greeks. Zeus predicts that the Greeks will be driven back to their ships, that Akhilleus will send his good friend Patroklos into battle, that Patroklos will be killed by Hektor, who will in turn be killed by Akhilleus. Finally, predicts Zeus, the Greeks will take Troy. For now, the Trojans are unstoppable, and led by Apollo, they advance to the Greek ships, which they begin to set on fire. Patroklos, who has been tending the injured Eurypylos, leaves the wounded warrior and returns to Akhilleus to convince Akhilleus to come to the Greeks' rescue.

Book Sixteen: A Ship Fired, a Tide Turned
Patroklos persuades Akhilleus to let him lead the Myrmidons in battle against the Trojans. Akhilleus lends Patroklos his armor, which protects him well—until he fails to heed Akhilleus's warning not to go too far. Sarpêdôn is killed and the Trojans are routed, but Akhilleus's good friend Patroklos is also killed when Apollo, Euphorbus and Hektor combine efforts against him. Fierce Hektor strips Patroklos of his armor.

Book Seventeen: Contending for a Soldier Fallen
Hektor grabs the armor that Patroklos had worn (Akhilleus's) and Greeks and Trojans fight over Patroklos's body. Glaukos (Trojan side) wants to trade Patroklos's body for that of Glaukos's dead friend, Sarpêdôn. (Actually, Glaukos is mistaken in thinking that the Greeks have Sarpêdôn's corpse.) Glaukos calls Hektor a coward and Hektor puts on the armor and goes out to fight for the body (which he plans to defile). Zeus covers the battlefield in a blanket of darkness. Akhilleus doesn't even know that Patroklos is dead until a runner is sent by the greater Aías and Menelaos to tell him. The Greeks finally rescue the body and carry it to the rear, but the Trojans advance again.

Book Eighteen: The Immortal Shield
Akhilleus is terribly upset over his friend Patroklos's death. His mother, Thetis, promises to get him new armor. When Akhilleus appears at the moat and lets out a war-cry, the Trojans stop advancing and hold a council of war. Hektor remains outside of the fortress walls and fights. Meanwhile, Thetis goes to the lame god, Hêphaistos (husband of Aphrodítê) and has him make a new shield for Akhilleus. Night falls.

Book Nineteen: The Avenger Fasts and Arms
On the fourth day of the battle, Akhilleus and Agamémnon are finally reconciled. Odysseus points out that the Greek soldiers should be fed before they are sent into the decisive battle they expect. Agamémnon gives gifts to Akhilleus and promises that he never laid a hand on Brisêis.

Book Twenty: The Ranging of Powers

Zeus gets the gods together and tells them that they are now free to step into the war. The battle starts and some gods side with the Greeks while others support the Trojans. (On the Greek side are: Hêra, Athêna, Poseidon, Hermês, Hêphaistos. On the Trojan side are: Arês, Apollo, Artemis, Lêto, Xánthos, Aphrodítê.) Akhilleus leads the Greek advance. Aineías fights Akhilleus, with Poseidon helping Aineías escape—even though Poseidon ordinarily sides with the Greeks—because Aineías is supposed to rule over the Trojan survivors when the war is over. Hektor attacks Akhilleus and is protected by Apollo, who hides Hektor in a cloud. Enraged, Akhilleus slaughters many Trojans, who are routed.

Book Twenty-One: The Clash of Man and River

Akhilleus has further exploits, including a battle with the river Xánthos (also called Skamánder). When Akhilleus drives half of the Trojan forces into the water, the god of the river is angered by the pollution of his waters and nearly drowns Akhilleus. Some of the gods come to Akhilleus's aid, and end up doing battle with other gods (Athêna with Arês, Athêna with Aphrodítê, Hêra with Artemis; Apollo declines to fight Poseidon). The Greeks are ahead and Apollo helps the Trojans get back behind the city walls by disguising himself as Agênor and leading Akhilleus on a chase.

Book Twenty-Two: Desolation Before Troy

Hektor is stranded outside the walls. Hektor's parents beg him to come back behind the safety of the city walls, but he refuses, insisting he will fight Akhilleus. Pretending to be Deiphobos, the brother to whom Hektor is closest, Athêna tricks Hektor into fighting Akhilleus. Hektor is killed by Akhilleus; the Greeks stab Hektor's body and Akhilleus drags the body behind his chariot.

Book Twenty-Three: A Friend Consigned to Death

Patroklos's ghost shows up and asks Akhilleus to bury him soon so that he will be accepted among the dead. The ghost also reminds Akhilleus of his own upcoming death in the Trojan War. Patroklos is buried and Akhilleus slays twelve Trojans he had captured earlier. Akhilleus presides over funeral games and is reconciled with the Greeks.

Book Twenty-Four: A Grace Given in Sorrow

Zeus decides that Hektor's body, which has been kept whole by Apollo, should be returned to his father, Priam. After Thetis informs her son of Zeus' wishes, Akhilleus treats Priam kindly and is reconciled with the gods. A funeral pyre is assembled and Hektor's burial is performed during a twelve-day cease-fire agreement.

Initiating Activities

Choose one or more of the following activities to help "prime" students for the *Iliad.* Some activities will supply background information that makes the story more comprehensible. Others will help students link the story with background experience and knowledge they already have.

1. **Anticipation Guide:** (See Novel Units Student Packet, Activity #1.): Students discuss their opinions of statements linked with themes they will meet in the story. For example:
   a) Revenge is sweet.
   b) It's not winning, but how you play the game that counts.
   c) Hell hath no fury like a woman scorned.
   d) All's fair in love and war.
   e) The ends justify the means.
   f) Saving face is important to me.
   g) I believe in "tit for tat."
   h) You should be concerned with the common good, above all.
   i) The good usually get their reward.
   j) Life is hard.
   k) Real men don't eat quiche.

2. **Video:**
   "Homer's Mythology: Tracing a Tradition" Part One looks at Homer's world; Part Two summarizes and comments on the *Iliad;* Part Three examines and outlines the *Odyssey.* Color. 36 minutes. Guidance Associates.
   "The Power of Myth" Joseph Campbell looks at the myths of the past and present. Color. 6 hours. Mystic Fire/Voyager.
   "Light of the Gods" This film traces the evolution of Greek art from the late 10th to the early 5th century, B.C.; filmed on location. Color. 28 minutes. National Gallery of Art.
   "Mythology: Gods and Goddesses" This is a pictorial survey of the Greek and Roman gods and goddesses retelling the myths of Zeus, Hêra, Poseidon, etc. Color. 41 minutes. Guidance Associates.

3. **Log:** Have students keep a response log as they read. On one side of the paper, the student summarizes each "Book" of the *Iliad.* On the other side of the paper, the student reacts to the episode in that Book with comments and questions ("I don't understand why Agamémnon...," "If I were Khriseis...," "Akhilleus reminds me of...").

4. **Brainstorming:** Tell students that the *Iliad* is a poem about the wrath of Akhilleus. Explain that students may be more familiar with the Latinized version of this name—Achilles—and of others they will meet in the story (see page 11, #18). Write the word *wrath* on the board and have students brainstorm ideas that come to mind, as you jot these ideas around the central word on the board. To jog students' thinking you might suggest—synonyms for wrath, common causes of wrath, consequences of wrath, famous examples of wrath, etc.

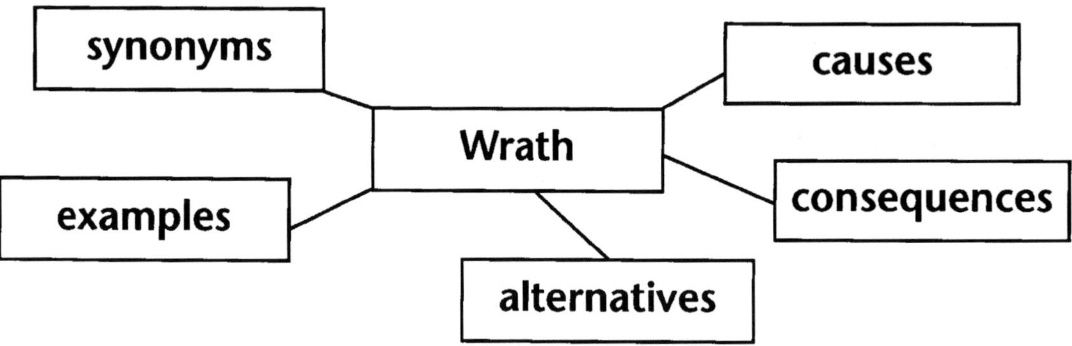

5. **Role Play:** Have small groups of students improvise skits based on the following situations (analogous to situations in the *Iliad).* After the parallel situation arises in the poem, have students discuss how their behavior in the role-play situations compares with the characters' behavior.
   - You're very angry with your young boss, who has started seeing your girlfriend/boyfriend.
   - Your friend is bent on getting revenge and you try to convince him/her that it's time to get over it.
   - Your friends need your help—but helping them means helping someone you can't stand, too.
   - You are engaged in some sort of contest (a chess match, a race, etc.). Just when you are about to win, someone tricks you and helps your opponent win.
   - Your best friend gets badly hurt—while helping you out.

6. **Freewrite:** Using the following sentence starters, write without stopping.
   - Myths are...
   - When you're telling a story out loud...
   - A good leader...
   - Revenge...
   - When soldiers are killed in battle...

- A hero...
- Loyalty...
- Saving face...
- Justice...
- Manliness...
- Tragedy....

7. **Discussion:**
   Of Gods and Goddesses—What is a myth? Are myths based on actual happenings? Who are your favorite gods and goddesses? What do you know about Zeus? Poseidon? Hêra? Aphrodítê? Athêna? Iris?
   Of the Oral Tradition—What are some examples of stories that were told for generation after generation before they were finally written down? Have you ever seen a storyteller in action—or told a story to a group yourself? What is hard about it? What do you like about it? What are some of the "memory devices" a storyteller might use? What are some ways a storyteller keeps the audience's attention?
   Of War—Why do wars begin? Do men and women tend to see war differently? What makes a good military leader? How would you define a "hero in battle"? How would you react if your brother or sister was about to go off to war?
   Of Loyalty—How much loyalty do you owe your friends? your boss? your nation? What sorts of "debts" do people rack up? Which debts do you think are important to repay?
   Of Shame and Guilt—What do these terms mean? How do they differ? Is it bad to feel shame or guilt? What sorts of things make us feel ashamed or guilty? What are some common responses?

8. **Geography:** Have students find the area in modern-day Turkey where Troy is believed to have been located. Also have them locate southern Greece (ruled by Agamémnon) and pinpoint Sparta (where Paris is supposed to have met Helen).

9. **Related Reading:** You might give students an overview of the story and/or some of the gods and goddesses they will meet in the story by having them read myths in which these figures appear. (To start, you might read aloud "The Trojan War" in *Bullfinch's Mythology.)*

10. **Preparation for Dramatization:** Tell students that they will be taking turns reading/acting out the story. Depending on your students' ability levels, you may want to to summarize preselected chapters. Some of the more confusing or less exciting chapters which you might consider summarizing are Books 2-5,

7-8, 10-11, 13-15, 20-21, and 23. For homework, students should consider what gestures/tones of voice they will use for the scene to be read aloud the next day. (Depending on how much time you have set aside for teaching the *Iliad,* you might form groups of students and divide the 24 Books—or a selected sample of these Books—among them.)

11. **Choral Reading:** Hand out copies of Akhilleus's speech condemning Agamémnon (in Book One, lines 175-190, "You thick-skinned, shameless, greedy fool! ... a prize I sweated for, and soldiers gave me!"). Have the class stand up and read it aloud together. Discuss what the scene reveals about the story. (What is Akhilleus like? Why is he angry at Agamémnon? Why is Agamémnon leading the Akhaians into battle against the Trojans?) Suggest that students keep their observations in mind as they read the poem.

12. **Pre-reading Summary:** Before your students read the *Iliad,* consider telling them the basic story (see the summary on pages 2-6), interspersing key lines from the translation throughout your telling. (Two or three students can be given lines to speak on cue as the story is told.)

13. Choose a **pivotal scene** from the story (e.g., Book Nine, where Akhilleus' friends appeal to him to put aside his differences with Agamémnon; Akhilleus refuses).
    a) Have students take turns reading the scene out loud, assigning about four lines per student.
    b) Ask students questions of varying difficulty about the scene. (e.g., "What three friends approach Akhilleus? Why? Why does Akhilleus refuse? Is there anything his friends could have said to make him accept?")
    c) Have small student groups work to rewrite the scene into script form, using contemporary language and adding stage directions that mention gestures, props, tone of voice, facial expressions, etc.
    d) Students decide as a group which of several hats best fits each character's personality. (Provide a box of yard-sale hats.)
    e) Have students block the scene (decide where actors will move, how they will speak their lines).
    f) Have each of the small groups enact the scene. Discuss differences in performance. (How does each performance lend a different interpretation to the meaning/emotions behind the lines?)
    g) Tell students to watch for this scene as they read the poem. (How well does their interpretation of the scene fit into the context of the story?)

    (**Note:** This can also be used as a post-reading activity.)

14. **Pronunciation:**
Tell students that
- a circumflex (^) indicates a long vowel sound; (Lêto is pronounced LAY-toe.)
- an accent mark (´) indicates stress; (Meneláos is pronounced men-a-LAY-os.)

15. **Vocabulary:**
Tell students that
- the terms "Akhaians," "Danáäns" and "Argives" are all used to apply to the Greeks in the *Iliad.* (These terms refer to the regions from which these people come. Remind students that Homer does not have a single word to refer to "the Greeks" because Greece was not a single country—as we know it—but an area of independent communities, the members of which shared a common language and religion.)
- the suffix *-ides* means "son of;" Kalkhas Thestorides means Kalkhas, son of Thestor.
- Some translators may refer to characters in the *Iliad* with Latinized names that are more familiar to readers than the Greek forms used by Fitzgerald in this edition.
  For example:

Fitzgerald's translation	**Latinized form**
Akhilleus	Achilles
Aías	Ajax
Patroklos	Patrocles

- the same god or man may be referred to by different names, even in the same translation of the *Iliad,* for example: Paris = Alexander.

16. **Graphic Aids:** Tell students that they will be meeting many mortals and gods/goddesses in the story. Suggest that they come up with their own symbols for each, to help them remember who's who (e.g., a bow and arrow for Apollo; running feet for Akhilleus, etc.). They might fill in a chart with the following headings as they read:

Name	Mortal	God/Goddess	Symbol	Does What	Greek/Trojan	Favors G/T

17. **Terms in Studying Greek Tragedy:** Have students look up definitions of the following: hubris, tragic/fatal flaw, catharsis, arret.

Book One: Quarrel, Oath, and Promise

Vocabulary *(numbers after words refer to line numbers)*

pyres (60) hekatombs (77) faction (206) poltroon (344)
ambrosial (607)

A recommended strategy for introducing these and other vocabulary words in the *Iliad:*
Before students have read Book One—

1) List the words and line numbers on the board. (Present the words in isolation.)
2) Have students predict what the words mean.
3) Have student volunteers read aloud the passage in which the word appears. (Present the words in context.)
4) Again have students predict what the words mean—and justify their guesses.
5) Have student volunteers consult a dictionary and read the definition aloud. (In other words—use a dictionary for verification. Students may need to do additional research to learn the definitions of certain terms such as "hekatombs"—lavish sacrifices to the gods.)

Discussion Questions

1. Why did Akhilleus quarrel with Agamémnon? (Agamémnon refused to return a captive girl, Khryseis, to her father. Apollo took the father's side and punished the Greeks. When Agamémnon finally let Khryseis go, he then took lovely Brisêis from Akhilleus.) Whose side would you take in this quarrel? How did their quarrel affect others? Have you ever been involved in an argument like theirs? Can you think of an argument that might take place today—that is somehow similar to the one in the *Iliad?* (For example, the coach of a basketball team quarrels with one of his key players.)
2. What sort of help did Akhilleus ask his mother for? (He asked Thetis to talk to Zeus about making Agamémnon "pay" by taking the Trojan side in the war against the Greeks.) Have you ever heard of a parent helping a child get revenge? Was that parent being a good parent—or being childish as well? Are you surprised that a goddess would get involved in "making someone pay"? What does this show you about the way the Greeks thought about their gods and goddesses?
3. "Odysseus,/the great tactician, led her to the altar, putting her in her father's hands..." (lines 505-507). What is your impression of Odysseus? (good mediator, strategist) How did the priest finally get his daughter, Khryseis, back from Agamémnon? (She was launched on a ship loaded with sacrificial beasts and wealth to appease Apollo.) How do you picture the reunion? Do you think the outcome would have been different if the priest hadn't been on Apollo's good side?

4. "Dear Mother, patience, hold your tongue,/no matter how upset you are. I would not see you battered, dearest" (lines 677-679). Why did Hêphaistos give this advice to his mother? (He didn't want Hêra to anger Zeus and get hurt.) What traits does Homer give the gods and goddesses? Are they like or unlike mortals in the way they relate to each other?
5. Which lines in Book One did you most enjoy reading aloud? Why?

Writing Activity: Write three newspaper headlines about events in Book One. Choose one headline and write the accompanying article. (For example: Plague Kills Hundreds of Greeks.

Research: Why does Nestor mention the centaurs (line 317)? Find out more about centaurs. What did they look like? Why did Theseus and others want to "break" centaurs?

Literary Analysis: *In Media Res*
Explain that the phrase *in media res* means "in the middle of things" and describes how the *Iliad*—and most epics—begin. An epic is a long narrative poem in elevated style that presents a series of episodes important to the history of a nation or race. The *Iliad* and the *Odyssey* are two of the most important folk epics.

Ask students to put the opening lines (1-8) in their own words. (Sample: "I'm asking you, inspiring Muse, to sing a story about Akhilleus and how his anger caused such a mess for the Greeks.") The story starts with a description of the argument between Akhilleus and Agamémnon. Ask students to describe the action the poem opens in the middle of. (The speaker is giving the listener the background of the quarrel between Agamémnon and Akhilleus—and explaining how Apollo got involved.)

Book Two: Assembly and Muster of Armies

Vocabulary

baldric (53)	harangue (84)	duplicity (131)	strategems (193)
beleager (283)	portent (357)	siege (431)	kites (462)
chines (503)	mien (559)	guise (954)	sortie (968)

Discussion Questions

1. How did Zeus act on Thetis's request to help Akhilleus? (He sent Agamémnon a false dream about the imminent fall of Troy so that Agamémnon was encouraged to go into battle without Akhilleus.) Why do you think Zeus listened to Thetis? Was he sympathetic? afraid of her? trying to placate her?

2. Explain what Agamémnon meant when he said that "Under great Zeus nine years have passed away...And yet the mission on which we came is far from being done." (lines 150-156). What caused the war? (For nine years, the Greeks have been trying to take Troy; a Trojan, Paris, had run off with the wife (Helen) of a Greek (Menelaos). Why do you think Agamémnon suddenly suggested that the Greeks give up on taking Troy? Who kept the Greeks from retreating, after all? (Nestor)
3. Why did Thersítês ask Agamémnon, "What have you got to groan about? What more/ can you gape after? Bronze fills your huts,/ bronze and the hottest girls"? (lines 256-259). What was his tone of voice? (whining, annoyed; The troops are angry with Agamémnon for getting them into this mess.) Do you think his criticism was justified? Who silenced him? (Odysseus) How? (struck him with a staff)
4. What portent did Odysseus remind the soldiers about? (A red serpent ate eight baby birds and their mother.) Why? (to pep up the men) How did he interpret that portent? (as a sign that they will take Troy on this the ninth year of the war) Did the men seem to believe in the portent? (yes) Do you believe in portents?
5. What animal did Agamémnon sacrifice? Why? (an Ox—so that Zeus would help keep death away) Can you think of other cultures throughout history that have made similar sacrifices?
6. What was the most vivid image in Book Two, for you?

Art Project: Illustrate the portent that appeared to the Greeks, as described by Odysseus in lines 357-371.

Literary Analysis: Catalogs

A characteristic common to epics such as the *Iliad* is the inclusion of catalogs or lists of warriors, ships, armies, etc. Point out the way Homer catalogs Greek and Trojan commanders and ships in Book Two. Ask students what the catalogs tell them about the relative size of the Greek and Trojan armies. (The Greeks outnumber the Trojans.)

Research: City States

Find out more about the Greek political system of city-states. How does Book Two make it clear that Greece at the time was not one unified country, but a coalition of states? (Homer describes the soldiers from each separate place.)

Book Three: Dueling for a Haunted Lady

Vocabulary

bane (12)	assail (30)	dispatched (139)	bellwether (234)
tactician (256)	mailed (299)	votive (322)	indemnity (345)
cuirass (395)	guise (468)	tribute (553)	

Discussion Questions

1. Who was the "Haunted Lady"? (Helen) How was she "haunted"? [Helen was greatly distressed by her role in the Greek-Trojan war; Aphrodítê made her go with Paris (Aléxandros) against her will.]
2. Whom did Paris agree to face in combat? (Menelaos) Do you think this was an act of bravery?
3. How did most of the Trojans feel about Helen? (They didn't blame her—Priam and others actually liked her—but many wished she would go back to Menelaos so that the war would end.) Do you think the war would have ended if she had said she would go back to her husband?
4. How did Aphrodítê manipulate the contest between Paris and Menelaos? Why? (She plucked Paris from the contest and sent him to his bedroom to keep him safe and reunite him with Helen.) What do you think the outcome would have been without her intervention?
5. What did Helen seem to feel regarding Paris? (aversion) Why did she go to his bedroom? (She was sent against her will by Aphrodítê.)
6. Helen asked Aphrodítê, "Is it because Menelaos has beaten Alexandros and/hateful though I am, would take me home...?" (lines 487-488). How did Helen seem to feel about Menelaos—and about herself? (loathing and self-loathing)
7. Why did the Greeks declare themselves the winners in the contest between Paris and Menelaos? (Paris had disappeared before the contest was over.) If you had been the judge, what would you have said?
8. "...being abhorred like death itself" (line 546): If the Trojans all hate Paris so much, why do you suppose they are they willing to fight a war he started by taking Helen?
9. What is one question Book Three raises in your mind?

Book Four: A Bowshot Bringing War

Vocabulary

amity (20)	exploit (109)	dolorous (118)	deflecting (154)
flange (182)	faceted (228)	malingering (270)	harangued (304)
melee (365)	tactician (397)	deferential (410)	whet (423)
inauspicious (461)	liege (468)	confluence (546)	warping (588)

Discussion Questions

1. How did Zeus say he thought the war should end? (with Troy being spared and Helen returning to Menelaos) Why did this annoy Hêra? (She sided with the Greeks.)
2. What did Athêna trick Pándaros into doing? (She tricked the archer into shooting Menelaos.) What was the result of Menelaos's injury? (He was only nicked, but the truce was broken.)
3. Agamémnon said to Diomêdês, "Weaker than he in war, the man he fathered, stronger in assembly" (lines 482-483). What tone of voice do you imagine he uses? (goading) What effect does Agamémnon hope to have on Diomêdês and the others listening? (He hopes to rouse them to fight.)
4. Can you think of one famous quote (or song lyric or line from a poem) that somehow applies to Book Four?

Book Five: A Hero Strives with Gods

Vocabulary

votary (11)	bereavement (27)	revetment (103)	fodder (236)
glutting (334)	brazen (389)	ichor (393)	poultice (461)
impious (464)	chaff (571)	sanctum (587)	insatiable (594)
formidable (643)	reprieve (793)	routed (795)	brocaded (836)
portent (845)	men-at-arms (847)	wantonly (868)	emanation (886)
scion (964)	truculence (1017)	anodyne (1028)	mantled (1034)

Discussion Questions

1. Which Greek warrior dominated the fighting? (Diomêdês) Did you feel sympathetic toward him?
2. Which gods and goddesses got involved in the battle—on which sides? (Athêna and Hêra on the side of the Greeks; Apollo, Aphrodítê and Arês on the side of the Trojans)
3. Which two gods were wounded? (Aphrodítê and Arês) Were you surprised? Was Zeus sympathetic about their wounds? (He sympathized with Aphrodítê, not with Arês.)

4. "I beg you not to leave me lying here for Danáäns to despoil. Defend me; afterward let me bleed away my life within your city" (lines 779-782). Who was pleading with whom? (Sarpêdôn was pleading with Hektor.) What was he worried about? (the possibility of his body being defiled by the Greeks) What does this show you about attitudes toward death? (Getting the body to the funeral, intact, was important; debasing the body was a great humiliation.)
5. Did you find any humor in Book Five?

Research: "concentered on the Gorgon's head" (line 844): Find an illustration of a gorgon and find out more about this beast.

Book Six: Interludes in Field and City

Vocabulary

interludes (title)	bastion (6)	tamarisk (44)	implacably (71)
cowed (85)	augur (86)	travail (89)	recoiled (121)
slander (193)	virile (220)	moiety (228)	progenitors (247)
slake (303)	supplication (362)	bereave (503)	dandle (552)

Discussion Questions

1. What did Hektor's brother suggest that Hektor instruct the Trojan women to do? (make offerings to Athêna so that she would control Diomêdês)
2. "...once in our hands not one should squirm away from death's hard fall! No fugitive, not even the manchild carried in a woman's belly" (lines 66-68): Who was speaking? (Hektor) What did this show you about him? (He was merciless, would kill even women, children, and unborn babies without pity.)
3. Why did Diomêdês and Glaukos decide not to fight each other? (They discovered their grandfathers had sworn friendship.) Would you say that this was the reverse of a family feud? What does it show you about Greek attitudes toward loyalty?
4. Do Paris and Hektor remind you of another pair of brothers—real or fictional?

Writing Activity: Helen wishes she were dead—"That day my mother gave me to the world/I wish *a hurricane blast had torn me away/to wild mountains, or into tumbling sea/to be washed under by a breaking wave...*"

Replace the italicized section with another image—either one that Homer might have used—or a contemporized one.

Book Seven: A Combat and a Rampart

Vocabulary

mace (10)	nape (13)	groveling (110)	carnage (135)
quails (149)	herald (222)	ruse (233)	callow (277)
millstone (316)	contenders (326)	chine (381)	abaft (394)
increment (431)	foundered (464)	cadavers (487)	rampart (521)
carls (527)	propitiate (538)	colloquy (554)	barter (563)
copious (566)			

Discussion Questions

1. With whom did Hektor duel? (Aías) What was the outcome? (a draw) Did you favor one or the other?
2. Why was a truce called? (so that burials could be done) Do you think it was honored by both sides?
3. Why did Paris (Aléxandros) refuse to give Helen back to the Greeks? Do you think he loved her? (It was probably more a matter of stubbornness and pride.)
4. What offer did the Trojans make to the Greeks? (They will give up the treasure Paris brought to Troy if that will end the war.) What was the Greeks' response? (refusal) Do you think the Trojans expected the Greeks to accept?
5. "All cries of mourning Priam forbade them" (lines 510-511). Why do you think Priam gave this order? What was done with the corpses on both sides? (put on a funeral pyre)
6. What do you see in your mind's eye as you read about "the gods arrayed with Zeus,/lord of the lightning flash, looked down" (line 529)? How would you show this scene if you were producing a film of the *Iliad?*

Book Eight: The Battle Swayed by Zeus

Vocabulary

contravene (7)	zenith (20)	panoply (46)	forfend (108)
incendiary (207)	frontlets (432)	emissary (461)	arbiter (485)
animus (509)	rancor (520)	prowess (536)	hoary (591)
striplings (591)	salutary (598)	tethering (619)	limpid (630)

Discussion Questions

1. How did Zeus feel about the gods participating in the fight between Trojans and Greeks? (ordered them not to)
2. What prediction did Zeus make about when Akhilleus would join the fight? (after Patroklos is killed)
3. "Now at the hands of Diomêdês there might soon have been a ruin of Trojans...had not the father of gods and men perceived it" (lines 147-150). How did Zeus step in, here? (gave off a bolt of lightning that spooked Diomêdês' horses) Did Zeus always favor that side? (no)
4. Why do you suppose Homer begins and ends this Book with a description of Dawn? How does he portray Dawn? (rosy-fingered woman in a lovely chair) How have other famous poets personified dawn?

Book Nine: A Visit of Emissaries

Vocabulary

emissaries (title)	craven (49)	formidable (61)	provender (85)
munificence (145)	precedence (195)	pillaging (339)	dowry (352)
tithes (362)	fledglings (395)	pre-empted (410)	hoary (448)
appease (472)	crypt (493)	illustrious (537)	parricide (560)
colonnade (573)	libation (607)	placate (608)	inveighed (626)
intercede (632)	amenable (640)	dolorous (665)	languished (676)
inexorable (695)	imploring (701)	malignant (730)	unappeasable (775)
scion (783)	perturbation (844)	deploy (860)	

Discussion Questions

1. "I lost my head, I yielded to black anger, but now I would retract it and appease him with all munificence" (lines 143-145). Who was speaking, here? (Agamémnon) What was he admitting? (He was wrong to anger Akhilleus.)
2. Who were the emissaries? (Phoenix, Odysseus, Aías) What was their mission? (to convince Akhilleus to help the Greeks)
3. Of what did the emissaries try to convince Akhilleus? (He should join the fighting.) What would you have said, if you were one of them? Did they succeed? (no)
4. What do you consider the most important decision anyone makes in Book Nine? Would you have made that decision?

Book Ten: Night in the Camp—a Foray

Vocabulary

foray (title)	myriad (14)	expedient (20)	havoc (58)
patronymic (76)	doleful (88)	whetted (149)	sentries (200)
dispelled (208)	carping (275)	quiver (287)	accoutered (303)
mettlesome (338)	brazen (357)	complied (363)	javelin (372)
rifling (381)	unwary (389)	fractious (449)	invocation (510)
bivouac (512)	canted (522)	baleful (539)	adept (542)
vaulted (585)	resourceful (626)		

Discussion Questions

1. Why did Odysseus and Diomêdês go out at night? (Nestor had suggested a reconnaisance patrol behind Trojan lines.)
2. How did Odysseus and Diomêdês trick Dolôn? (They convinced him they would spare his life if he would give them the Trojan battle plans.) Do you think this was a "cheap trick"—or is "all fair in love and war"?
3. What happened to Dolôn? (Diomêdês killed him.) Did you feel sorry for him?
4. Where did Odysseus and Diomêdês get the fabulous horses? (They killed King Rhêsos and several of his men and took his horses.)
5. "Astern upon his ship, Odysseus hung the bloodstained gear of Dolôn" (lines 630-631). Why? (as an offering to Athêna)
6. Did any part of Book Ten make you feel sad or angry?

Writing Activity: Write a letter to Agamémnon, with advice on how to get a better night's sleep.

Literary Analysis: Homeric Epithet
A **Homeric Epithet** is an adjectival phrase so often repeated in connection with a person or thing that it almost becomes a part of the name, as "Odysseus, the resourceful man" (line 614). Have students make a list of other epithets they find in the *Iliad.*

Book Eleven: Prowess and Wounds of Akhaians

Vocabulary

prowess (title)	presages (30)	scabbard (33)	irrepressible (55)
decreeing (88)	stripling (112)	infamy (162)	bereft (186)
laggards (206)	herald (214)	brunt (236)	thews (270)
beeves (281)	lacerated (307)	adversaries (341)	rent (351)
respite (370)	clairvoyant (373)	impervious (402)	swoon (405)
patriarch (422)	vaunting (432)	ordeal (435)	pike (440)
bandying (464)	deploy (472)	navel (483)	prodigies (576)
dun (631)	oracle (920)		

Discussion Questions

1. Who wounded Diomêdês? (Paris) What happened to Odysseus and Makhâôn? (They were wounded.)
2. What was Zeus's message to Hektor? (Stay out of the battle until Agamémnon is hurt.) How did he get the message to the Trojan? (via Iris)
3. Who wounded Agamémnon? (Koôn) What did Hektor do, as a result? (joined the fray)
4. Why did Akhilleus send Patroklos to Nestor? (to ask about the wounded man Nestor was tending) Do you think he was worried about Patroklos's safety? Why do you suppose he didn't go himself?
5. What did Nestor advise Patroklos to tell Akhilleus? (try to convince him to join the battle, or at least to let Patroklos lead the Myrmidons into battle against the Trojans, wearing Akhilleus' armor)
6. "Noble Patroklos, there will be no longer any defensive line of Akhaians" (lines 952-953): Who was speaking? (Eurypylos) According to his report, which side had the upper hand, at that point? (Trojans)
7. How did Patroklos help Eurypylos? (Eurypylos was wounded.) What does this show you about Patroklos? (compassionate; He came to Eurypylos' aid even though he was on his way to give Akhilleus counsel from Nestor.)
8. Which character in Book Eleven did you most want to protect?

Literary Analysis: Hubris

Hubris is extreme pride which results in the misfortune of the protagonist of a tragedy. It is the particular form of tragic flaw which results from excessive pride, ambition, and overconfidence. Hubris causes the protagonist to break a moral law or ignore a divine warning. Ask students whether they feel that Akhilleus, Hektor, and/or Agamémnon display hubris.

Book Twelve: The Rampart Breached

Vocabulary

breached (title) | unsacked (12) | erosion (20) | trident (33)
shunted (35) | rout (46) | auxiliaries (69) | impaled (75)
deployed (100) | prodigiously (171) | nestlings (245) | revetments (287)
parapet (295) | shaft (449) | pittance (486) | visage (517)

Discussion Questions

1. Who led the Trojans as they pressed on against the Greeks? (Hektor)
2. What was Poulydamas's advice about crossing the moat? (go on foot) Why do you think he gave that advice? Was his advice followed? (yes)
3. Of what portent did Poulydamas remind Hektor? Why? (He brought up the incident where the eagle dropped the snake which ate the birds to convince Hektor that the sign meant the army should retreat.) What was Hektor's response?(He ignored this advice.)
4. "Lightly Hektor handled it alone, for Zeus...made it a trifling weight for him" (lines 501-503): How did Zeus help Hektor? (picked up a boulder to break down the door) What happened next? (The Trojans leaped through the gate; Greeks ran out to their ships.)
5. Would you say that the tension was high at the end of Book Twelve—or was there a "lull" in the story here?

Book Thirteen: Assault on the Ships

Vocabulary

nomads (7) | enthralled (13) | seer (80) | shirk (111)
impetus (156) | consort (176) | compact (180) | verdure (204)
kindled (236) | revered (247) | carnage (255) | slack (261)
ambuscade (322) | nape (328) | bane (337) | vulnerable (363)
belied (410) | deflect (423) | concentric (463) | brawny (467)
hobbled (497) | pillar (499) | ardor (620) | winnower (671)
hewing (699) | vileness (709) | insolence (725) | surfeit (727)
wary (742) | retribution (755) | visionary (762) | pelting (824)
gittern (839) | milksop (894) | clamorous (917) | scourge (933)
glut (955)

Discussion Questions

1. What is the "assault on the ships" mentioned in the title? (Trojans attack the Greek ships.)
2. Who mobilized the Greeks, despite Zeus's order that no gods interfere in the mortals' combat? (Poseidon)
3. What two warriors led the Greeks? (the two Aías)
4. Why was Poseidon so enraged when Hektor killed Amphímakhos? (Amphimakhos was Poseidon's grandson.) Who did Poseidon protect, afterwards? (Idómeneus, King of Krete)
5. "...you bad-luck charm, so brave to look at, woman-crazed, seducer" (lines 884-885); Who was speaking to whom? (Hektor was berating his brother, Paris, for not participating in the battle that began because of his actions.) What attitude is revealed here? (scorn)
6. If you could ask Zeus one question about his behavior in Book Thirteen, what would it be?

Writing Activity: Apparently "milksop" was an insulting term (see line 894). Consider some of the insults that Homer's characters hurl at each other. Write a Homeric insult of your own.

Book Fourteen: Beguilement on Mount Ida

Vocabulary

beguilement (title)	caldron (7)	burly (14)	promontories (41)
advent (44)	impregnable (61)	bulwark (62)	harried (66)
moor (86)	assent (152)	odious (181)	bourne (227)
expedient (239)	girdle (247)	talisman (251)	venerable (272)
corroding (307)	impetuous (371)	subjugated (396)	parry (435)
élan (468)	flank (583)		

Discussion Questions

1. What was Agamémnon's plan? (launch the ships, retreat) What did Odysseus think of it? (He considered the plan cowardly.) Do you agree?
2. How did Hêra trick Zeus? (She seduced him and put him to sleep.) Why? (to help the Greeks, against Zeus's orders)
3. What other god did Hêra tell Sleep to urge to help the Greeks? (Poseidon)
4. How was Hektor injured? (wounded by a stone hurled by Telemônian Aías)

5. "Go tell Ilioneus' father and his mother for me, Trojans, to mourn him in their hall" (lines 565-566): Who is speaking? In what tone? (Pênéleos is jeering.)
6. Which character do you feel sorriest for in Book Fourteen? Why?

Writing Activity: Suppose you were writing a story that takes place in today's world, based on some of the events and characters in the *Iliad.* Write the (G-rated) scene in which the modern-day Hêra comes up with a plan for distracting Zeus.

Book Fifteen: The Lord of Storm

Vocabulary

connived (31)	august (45)	mailed (67)	remit (87)
pandemonium (161)	gall (215)	insolent (215)	irks (244)
unappeasable (253)	conjure (273)	demurring (275)	peregrine (277)
supine (279)	sated (369)	haunches (433)	salve (457)
ignoble (572)	valorous (607)	obliquely (625)	carnivores (684)
slaver (702)	constrained (766)	nebulous (778)	recompense (832)

Discussion Questions

1. "I should not wonder if this time you will be the first to catch it, a whip across your shoulders for your pains!" (lines 18-20): Who was threatening whom? Why? (Zeus was angry at Hêra for tricking him and getting Hektor wounded.)
2. What message did Zeus have Iris give Poseidon? (withdraw from the mortals' battle)
3. What prediction did Zeus make about Patroklos and Hektor? (Akhilleus will send Patroklos into battle; Patroklos will be killed by Hektor, who will in turn be killed by Akhilleus.)
4. Which god was leading the Trojans in their advance on the Greek ships? (Apollo) What did they do once they reached the ships? (set them on fire)
5. "Eurypylos, I cannot linger with you here, much as you need me" (lines 461-463): Who was speaking? (Patroklos) Why did he have to leave? (He returned to Akhilleus to try to convince him to come to the aid of the Greeks.)
6. What is the last image we are left with at the end of Book Fifteen? (Aías knocking down Trojans as they try to leap onto the Greek ships)
7. If you were illustrating one incident from Book Fifteen, which one would you choose to show?

Book Sixteen: A Ship Fired, a Tide Turned

Vocabulary

oracle (42)	beacon (36)	vagabond (68)	berserk (87)
smote (146)	daub (309)	repelled (353)	shipwrights (561)
sultry (565)	stanched (600)	suppliant (661)	augment (744)
moil (744)	mantling (764)	attentive (774)	resplendent (809)
guise (822)	semblance (826)	jeered (855)	agape (923)
immutable (981)			

Discussion Questions

1. What did Patroklos persuade Akhilleus to do? (to let Patroklos lead the Myrmidons in battle against the Trojans)
2. What did Akhilleus lend Patroklos, for protection? (his armor)
3. "...and the two men fought over the body like two mountain lions (lines 867-868): Who were the men? (Patroklos and Hektor) How were they like lions? (Both fought over Kebríonês body, the way lions fight over a deer.)
4. How did Patroklos die? (He failed to heed Akhilleus's warning not to go too far and was killed when Apollo, Euphorbus, and Hektor attacked him.) Do you think he was afraid to die?
5. How did Hektor treat Patroklos's body? (put his heel on it) Why? (to defile it)
6. Patroklos exhorted the soldiers to "remember courage" (line 318). Do you think most of the soldiers described in Book Sixteen are brave? How else might you explain why some of these soldiers are risking their lives?

Literary Analysis: Catharsis

According to Aristotle, representations of suffering and death in literature paradoxically leave the audience feeling relieved rather than depressed. This is called **catharsis.** How do you feel after reading the account of Patroklos's death?

Writing Activity

Homer describes repeatedly how "darkness veiled his eyes." Make a list of euphemisms for death used by Homer—and others. (Try creating a few of your own.)

Book Seventeen: Contending for a Soldier Fallen

Vocabulary

heifer (6), harrowed (40), umbrage (76), intractable (81)
audacity (87), despoiled (135), scavenging (170), insolent (191)
platoon (212), presage (225), blanch (227), besiegers (249)
requisitioning (251), complied (275), glade (315), vigilant (429)
pelting (615), ravening (626), gristle (638), void (795)
leverage (809), conflagration (836)

Discussion Questions

1. What happened to the armor Akhilleus had lent Patroklos? (Hektor grabbed it.)
2. What trade did Glaukos propose? (Patroklos's body for that of Glaukos's friend, Sarpêdôn)
3. Who covered the battlefield in darkness? (Zeus) Why, do you suppose?
4. How did Akhilleus find out that his friend Patroklos was dead? (A runner was sent by the greater Aías and Menelaos to tell Akhilleus.)
5. "From the Trojan mass a cry broke out, as they perceived the Akhaians lifting the body" (lines 817-818): What happened next? (The Trojans pressed on but didn't dare try to get the body when they saw the two Aiases; the Greeks successfully retrieved Patroklos's body.)
6. How do you think Antílokhos broke the sad news about Patroklos to Akhilleus? What do you predict Akhilleus's reaction was? (probably rage, sorrow)

Literary Analysis: Homeric Simile

A **simile** is a comparison containing the words "like" or "as." (Example: "My hands are like ice.") A **Homeric simile** is an epic simile, an unusually elaborate comparison, that extends through a number of lines.

> Sample: "Aías/extending his broad shield above Patroklos, stood as a lion will above his cubs/when a hunting party comes upon the beast/in underbrush, leading his young." (lines 147-150)

Have students suggest other comparisons Homer might have made, here. Then have students find other similes in Book Seventeen.

Book Eighteen: The Immortal Shield

Vocabulary

wayward (15)	spoils (31)	storied (50)	extremity (112)
abstained (145)	impale (204)	illustrious (212)	moat (248)
sentries (347)	tactics (364)	meandering (373)	prophecy (378)
progeny (420)	thrall (497)	crucibles (541)	arbiter (576)
parleying (609)	vintagers (653)	artisan (661)	garlands (685)

Discussion Questions

1. How did Thetis comfort Akhilleus? What did she promise him? (She promised to get him new armor.)
2. "You'll be swift to meet your end, child, as you say: your doom comes close on the heels of Hektor's own" (lines 108-109): Who made this prediction? (Thetis) Was Akhilleus frightened by it? (no)
3. What did the Trojans do when Akhilleus appeared on the wall and let out a war-cry? (stopped and held a war council) What did Hektor do? (remained outside of the fortress walls to fight)
4. Who was Hêphaistos? (lame god, husband of Aphrodítê) What did he make for Akhilleus? (a new shield)
5. What did you like about Book Eighteen?

Book Nineteen: The Avenger Fasts and Arms

Vocabulary

carrion (28)	abjure (85)	vexation (91)	victualing (187)
sate (199)	conciliate (203)	savory (349)	greaves (405)
sloth (457)			

Discussion Questions

1. "I feel the dread that while I fight black carrion flies may settle on Patroklos' wounds" (lines 27-29): Who was worried? About what? (Akhilleus was worried that Patroklos's body would decompose before he had a proper funeral.) How did Thetis comfort him? (She promised to keep the flesh intact indefinitely.)

2. "I drop my anger now...Come, send your long-haired Akhaians into combat" (lines 76-78): What was Akhilleus saying? (He was no longer angry and would help the Greeks.) To whom? (Agamémnon) Would you say he was apologizing? What was Agamémnon's response? (pleased) Did he accept responsibility for his actions? (He said he wasn't to blame; Zeus and Fate and Fury put Folly in his mind.) What was the Akhaians' reaction? (They were overjoyed.) Why? (to have the great Akhilleus back on their side)
3. What did Odysseus suggest the soldiers needed before going into the decisive battle? (food)
4. What gifts did Agamémnon give Akhilleus? (tripods, horses, women, gold) What did he promise—regarding Brisêis? (that he had never lain with her) Do you believe him?
5. Choose one line from Book Eighteen that strikes you somehow—and explain why.

Writing Activity: You are Agamémnon. Write a poem or letter of apology/acceptance to Akhilleus.

Book Twenty: The Ranging of Powers

Vocabulary

partisans (42)	unavailing (145)	intimation (151)	embroil (157)
conclave (168)	reverberated (184)	omnipotent (276)	bandy-legged (306)
gullible (336)	traversing (369)	naiad (435)	cleft (455)
vented (517)	beseeching (540)	inert (554)	glens (568)
mire (582)			

Discussion Questions

1. What instructions did Zeus give the gods about interfering in the mortals' combat, in Book Twenty? (He said they could interpose at that point.)
2. Who did Poseidon help escape? (Aineías) Why was this surprising? (Aineías was Trojan and Poseidon usually sided with the Greeks.) Why did he provide this aid? (Aineis was fated to rule over the Trojan survivors.)
3. How did Apollo protect Hektor after Hektor attacked Akhilleus? (He hid Hektor in a cloud.) What was Akhilleus's response? (rage; Akhilleus slaughtered many Trojans.)
4. "No moderate temper, no mild heart was in this man, but harsh and deadly purpose" (lines 537-539): Who is Homer describing as heartless? (Akhilleus)

5. There are many bloody descriptions of death in this Book. Which ones do you find the most gut-wrenching? Why do you suppose Homer goes into such revolting detail?

Research: Iphítiôn was "born by a naiad" (line 435). Find out more about the mythical naiads.

Book Twenty-One: The Clash of Man and River

Vocabulary

ford (1)	hurly-burly (12)	cowered (29)	dispatch (56)
balks (69)	shoals (118)	avenged (156)	contender (175)
ambitextrous (192)	gloating (215)	waywardness (250)	wantonly (258)
marshal (258)	arrogant (262)	bellowing (279)	mattock (303)
purling (306)	buffeted (316)	travail (321)	counsel (342)
directive (351)	channels (364)	barrow (378)	turbulence (380)
slackening (387)	galingale (411)	torrid (415)	interpose (437)
lunged (458)	baleful (483)	incensed (483)	swoon (497)
derisively (498)	impregnable (523)	vile (528)	coddle (534)
ephemeral (542)	fisticuffs (580)	harrowing (609)	refuge (624)
tangent (646)			

Discussion Questions

1. Who did battle with the river Skamánder? (Akhilleus) What was the outcome? (The god of the river got angry when Akhilleus drove Trojans into the water; it nearly drowned Akhilleus; other gods helped rescue Akhilleus.)
2. Which gods came to Akhilleus's aid—and ended up fighting each other? (Athêna fought Arês, Hêra fought Artemis.) Are you surprised to see gods in combat with each other?
3. How did Apollo help the Trojans get back behind the city walls—away from Akhilleus? (He disguised himself as a Trojan and led Akhilleus on a chase while the Trojans took the opportunity to escape him.) Does this deception remind you of other incidents from the *Iliad*—or from other stories you have heard?
4. "all whose legs had saved them now took cover, in hot haste entering the city" (lines 708-709): Who ran to safety? (frightened Trojans)
5. Would you say that the river becomes a character in Book Twenty-One? Can you think of other stories/poems in which a river becomes more than simply a part of the setting?

Book Twenty-Two: Desolation Before Troy

Vocabulary

quarry (16)	hanks (93)	parley (153)	cleft (172)
harry (223)	forestall (245)	unappeased (258)	glutting (315)
shank (326)	conspicuous (375)	encampment (404)	ransom (416)
tripod (521)			

Discussion Questions

1. Who was stranded outside the city walls? (Hektor) Did he panic? (no) How did his parents try to get him back inside? (They begged him to think of them, not bring them—and his wife—grief by getting killed.)
2. How did Athêna trick Hektor into fighting Akhilleus? (She assumed the form and voice of his brother; prodded him by saying "Come, we'll stand and take him.")
3. How was Hektor killed? (Akhilleus first slashed him through the neck, leaving his windpipe and voice intact; Hektor begged Akhilleus not to defile his body and the scornful Akhilleus refused.) How was his body defiled? Why? (Angry Akhilleus wanted to further humiliate Hektor and the Trojans; Akhilleus stripped the body and dragged it, head down, behind the chariot.)
4. Were you rooting more for Hektor or for Akhilleus? How did you feel when Hektor was killed?
5. "How I could wish I never had been born!/ Now under earth's roof to the house of Death you go your way and leave me here, bereft" (lines 568-570): Who is crying out here? (Hektor's wife) Do you feel sorry for her?

Book Twenty-Three: A Friend Consigned to Death

Vocabulary

consigned (title)	lament (16)	engulfed (94)	forage (131)
staunch (133)	ungelded (170)	sheathed (194)	unguent (196)
anointing (214)	blustering (232)	arena (317)	astuteness (363)
yoked (403)	tawny (460)	gully (480)	discus (493)
circuit (534)	versatile (809)	rills (822)	warp (875)
stalwart (961)	plummeted (1005)		

Discussion Questions

1. What did Patroklos's ghost ask Akhilleus to do? (bury him soon) How do you imagine his tone of voice? Onstage, how might you handle this scene where the ghost addresses Akhilleus (lines 80-108)? Would you show the ghost?

2. "Fire will devour twelve noble sons of Troy along with you, but I will not restore Hektor to Priam; he shall not be eaten by fire but by wild dogs" (line 208-211): What was Akhilleus's boast? (Akhilleus promised that Patroklos's funeral rites would be conducted properly—including the slaying of 12 Trojans who had been captured earlier for that reason; Akhilleus vowed that Hektor's body would be defiled.) Did he make good on his promise? (Akhilleus did slay the 12 Trojans and oversee Patroklos's burial.)
3. What did Patroklos's ghost predict about Akhilleus's death? (that Akhilleus would die in the Trojan war)
4. What sorts of funeral games were held when Patroklos was buried? (fist-fighting; chariot races, duels with spears, heaving iron—shot put; shooting at a dove with bow and arrow; javelin-throwing; running; wrestling) Who presided over these? (Akhilleus)
5. If you were enacting a five-minute dramatization of Book Twenty-Three, what would you show—and what would you leave out? Why?

Writing Activity: What sort of friendship do you imagine Akhilleus and Patroklos had? Describe Akhilleus' memory of a time he shared with Patroklos.

Book Twenty-Four: A Grace Given in Sorrow

Vocabulary

boon (3)	buoyant (7)	laceration (24)	piqued (34)
malevolent (39)	barbarous (48)	insensate (64)	veering (227)
whelps (304)	maneuverable (321)	courier (353)	pinion (388)
prudence (429)	affable (436)	dismembered (487)	discretion (520)
supplication (557)	exile (574)	stint (602)	felicity (644)
khiton (694)	suspend (800)	allay (803)	palisaded (806)

Discussion Questions

1. Why did Priam go to Akhilleus? (to plead with Akhilleus for the body of his son, Hektor) Do you think Priam was afraid? What "affable god" assisted Priam (line 436) (Hermês) How did Akhilleus treat Priam? (respectfully, took pity; acknowledged Priam's pain; told him to sit down and rest; got annoyed and told the old man not to vex him as he intended to yield Hektor in his own good time)
2. Who pressured Akhilleus to return Hektor's body to the Trojans? (Hektor's father—Priam; Akhilleus's mother—Thetis—also told him the gods were angry and wanted the body released.) What do you think was the main reason

Akhilleus gave up the body, in the end? Had he changed? (He did seem to have softened when he showed compassion for Priam)

3. How do you like the way Homer ends the *Iliad?* How/where would you have ended it? Are you surprised that Akhilleus agreed to suspend the war during the funeral? Homer has told us that this war has been going on for ten years. Are you surprised that he doesn't end by showing the outcome? Do you think the Greeks will succeed in taking Troy? Why do you suppose Homer stops short of this point in the story?

Writing Activity: Write a memorial poem for Hektor (by Priam) or one for Patroklos (by Akhilleus).

Further Reading

Boardman, John, Jasper Griffin, and Oswyn Murray, Eds.,*The Oxford History of the Classical World,* 1986. (good introductory essay on Homer)

Camps, W.A., *An Introduction to Homer,* 1980.

Chadwick, John, *The Decipherment of Linear B,* 1960. (description of life in pre-Homeric civilization)

Clarke, Howard, *Homer's Readers,* 1981. (what is known about the circumstances under which Homer wrote)

Graves, Robert, *The Greek Myths.*

Griffin, Jasper, *Homer,* 1980.

Griffin, Jasper, *Homer on Life and Death,* 1980.

Hogan, James C., *A Guide to the Iliad,* 1979. (good commentary on the *Iliad* based on Fitzgerald's translation and with a foreword by him)

Kirk, G. S., *Homer and the Oral Tradition,* 1976.

McDonald, W. A., *Progress Into the Past.* (about the unearthing fo the bronze age city at the site of Troy)

Steiner, George and Robert Fagles, *Homer: A Collection of Critical Essays,* 1962.

Wace, Alan J. B. and Frank H. Stubbings, *A Companion to Homer,* 1962.

Wood, Michael, *In Search of the Trojan War.* (archaeological background)

Internet Address (helpful for background information on the *Iliad):*
http://www.usask.ca/classics/CourseNotes/HomSummary.html

Post-reading Extension Activities and Assessment Ideas

Writing

1. Write an essay about how one of the following themes is developed throughout the *Iliad:* manliness, pride, revenge, sacrifice, compassion, solidarity, war and peace. Provide specific examples and speculate about what Homer is saying about the theme you choose.

2. Compare and contrast the *Iliad* and the *Odyssey.* Include these points of comparison:

	Iliad	*Odyssey*
setting		
plot		
main characters		
themes		
tragedy vs. comedy		

   Your response might be in (a) chart form, (b) essay form, or (c) humorous form (e.g., an article of fiction for the make-believe book, *Homer for Dummies* on how to sound literate at a cocktail party by revealing your knowledge of the differences between the *Iliad* and the *Odyssey).*

3. Write an essay about what an epic is—and why the *Iliad* is considered one of the finest examples of the form. (Start with a reference book such as *A Handbook to Literature,* ed. C. Hugh Holman. Then read some critical commentary, such as *A Companion to Homer,* by Alan J.B. Wace and Frank H. Stubbings.)

4. Compare and contrast the *Iliad* and another piece of literature about war (such as Stephen Crane's *The Red Badge of Courage).* Are there common themes? similar conflicts? similar characters?

5. Analyze the view of women as property in the *Iliad.*

6. Write an essay that describes what you learned about the norms governing human relationships in the society described by Homer. For example, what does the *Iliad* reveal about gift-giving, supplication, privileges, etc.? Provide specific examples.

7. Have one of the characters write to Dear Abby about a problem he/she is having. For example, what complaint might Hektor's wife have about Hektor—or Hêra, about Zeus? Have a partner write Abby's answer.

8. Create a newspaper based on events of one Book in the *Iliad.* Include weather, news headlines and stories, obituaries, an editorial, a social page, a sports page, personals/classified ads, a calendar of events (Several student groups might participate in a cooperative project, each covering one Book of the *Iliad.)*

9. Create a game based on the *Iliad.* Possibilities:

   a) crossword puzzle
   b) word search
   c) "Trivial Pursuit" (e.g., Q: Who was Hektor's best friend? A: Patroklos)
   d) "Jeopardy" (Categories might include: Gods & Goddesses; Greek Women; Weapons; etc.)
   e) "Concentration" game (Put character names on one set of cards, descriptions of the characters on another set of cards; the player who is "up" places all cards face down and then turns over two cards. If the cards match, s(he) gets another turn. Continue until all matches are made.)
   e) "Wheel of Fortune" (Students make up clues and block out some of the letters in the answer. Two other students base their guesses on the clue provided. Sample clue: Zeus's prediction:

      Gameboard Letters:

      __E __EE_S _I__ T__E T___

      Answer: The Greeks will take Troy.)
   f) "Win, Lose, or Draw" or Charades (The student who is up draws or mimes a character or event in the *Iliad.* Other students try to guess what/who is being depicted.)

10. Create new titles for some of the Books.

11. Take a look at a soap opera summary in a local newspaper. Using this as your model, choose one of the Books, give it an appropriate "soap opera" title, and summarize it.

12. Choose one of the statements included in the Anticpation Guide (pre-reading activity #1). Explain how that statement applies to the *Iliad.*

13. Write an essay in which you defend or refute the following thesis: *Akhilleus suffers from a tragic flaw.*

14. Student essays sometimes contain "bloopers"—erroneous statements that are as funny as they are incorrect. Create a set of bloopers that might result from misconceptions about the *Iliad.*

    Sample: Question: How did Zeus get his message to Poseidon? (See Book Fifteen, lines 67-68.)

    "Iris will go amid the mailed Akhaians
    with my word to Poseidon..."

    Blooper: He had Iris put it in the mail.

    Correct Answer: He sent Iris out to the Greek camp with a message for Poseidon.

    Have a partner correct the bloopers by providing the correct paraphrase.

Language Study

1. Make a list of your favorite "Homeric similes" from the *Iliad.*
2. Make a list of common words or expressions that have their origins in the names of Greek gods or goddesses found in the *Iliad.* For example—aphrodisiac—Aphrodítê; hector—to bully or harass—Hektor; hermetically—Hermês. (A helpful resource for this project: *Dictionary of Word Origins* by Joseph T. Shipley.)

Drama

1. Choose your favorite scene from the *Iliad,* create some simple costumes/props, and stage a "tableau" (with actors frozen in place). Photograph group tableaux and create a bulletin board display. (Some scenes that would work well include: Book Three—where Helen identifies various Greeks for Priam; Book Four—where Athêna tricks Pándaros into shooting an arrow at Menelaos; Book Ten—where Odysseus and Diomêdês trick Dolôn into spilling the beans; Book Eighteen—where Thetis asks Hêphaistos to make armor for Akhilleus; Book Twenty-Two, where Hektor's parents beg him to come back inside the city walls.)
2. *Wishbone* is a half-hour program on PBS which introduces young people to the classics. The action flashes back and forth between scenes from the classic and analogous present-day scenes from the life of a family (including the family's dog, Wishbone). Using the structure of this TV show as your model, create a half-hour dramatic presentation that shows a few key scenes from the *Iliad*—and a few scenes from today's world, in which characters are going through some of the same things as characters in the *Iliad.* (Write an actual *Wishbone* script, if you like.)

Art

1. Illustrate one of the weapons or pieces of armor described in the poem, such as the shield made by Hêphaistos or the helmet worn by Hektor when he said good-bye to his wife and infant son.

2. Create a mobile of items from the *Iliad* (e.g., Akhilleus's shield and Nestor's cup). Describe the significance of each item. This may done by writing a one-paragraph caption to be posted on the wall near the display, or by labeling each item on the back. (The second method would work well if you create a paper plate mobile by cutting a paper plate in half and suspending paper cut-outs from the straight edge by different lengths of thread.)

3. Create a symbol for each of the major characters and gods in the *Iliad.* For example, Zeus's symbol might be a thunderbolt and Akhilleus's might be his shield.

4. Draw a political cartoon that implies a parallel between a current event and the the *Iliad.* For example, President Clinton might be portrayed as Agamémnon and Newt Gingrich might be drawn as Akhilleus in a cartoon that spoofs the ongoing conflict between these two politicians. (See Current Events Activity #2 for an example.)

Research

1. Find out more about megalomaniacal Heinrich Schliemann and his unearthing of a bronze age city in Northwest Turkey at the site of Troy, in 1870. What evidence was discovered of a civilization like that described in the poems of Homer—poems that describe a much earlier age than the one in which Homer lived? Is it true that Schliemann had his wife dress up in Helen's jewelry? What controversy arose concerning "Priam's treasure"? How did it end up in Russia? What is the current status of international negotiations over the treasure? If you have access to the Internet, you might start by tapping into the following: http://www.usask.ca/classics/CourseNotes/HomBA.html

2. Find photographs of artwork that was created during the Greek Bronze Age (the time period Homer's poem describes). You can view vases, urns, jewelry, etc. on the Internet.

3. Research life in Greece during Homer's time. (What was the life of a bard probably like? What was it like to be a woman at that time?)

4. Choose your favorite Greek god from the *Iliad.* Examine how that god is portrayed in different myths. (For example, you might take a look at the Epic Cycle, a series of shorter epics—which post-dates Homer—designed to fill in the parts of the Trojan saga omitted by Homer.) See how Akhilleus is portrayed there. Find out what scholars have to say about why "Akhilleus's heel" is not mentioned in the *Iliad.* (Did Homer choose to ignore the traditional story of how Thetis dipped him in the River Styx? Was Homer ignorant of the story? Was the story simply told after Homer's time?)

5. Write an essay supporting the following thesis: Zeus and Akhilleus mirror one another in interesting ways.

6. Choose one of the gods or goddesses in the *Iliad* and describe him/her. How does he/she display human qualities? How does he/she interfere in the lives of the mortals? Does he/she provide moments of comedy? Is he/she used by Homer to underline the signficance of a particular event? (e.g., the emphasis on Sarpêdôn's death lent by Zeus's grief)

Current Events

1. Examine how one of the themes or characters in the *Iliad* pervades popular culture and literature. For example, list recent headlines that refer to incidents or characters in the *Iliad.* Which contemporary film/fiction writers have borrowed from the *Iliad?*

2. Create a bulletin board display of recent news stories that somehow tie in with themes or events in the *Iliad*—and write a caption that explains the connection in each case.

   For example: Here is a headline from the *Washington Post* (11/16/95) concerning the government shut-down:

   Underlying Gingrich's Stance Is His Pique About President

   The article goes on to suggest that Gingrich helped to bring about the shut-down—a political crisis that affected thousands of workers across the nation—in part due to his anger at being ignored by President Clinton during a trip they had recently taken on the same plane (to Israeli Prime Minister Yitzhak Rabin's funeral, following his assassination). The following day, an article stated that

"President Clinton gladly assumed a statesmanlike pose. 'I can tell you this,' he said. 'If it would get the government open, I'd be glad to tell him I'm sorry.' " However, the President rejected the House's plan for ending the shutdown—a plan supported by 48 Democrats from Clinton's own party, as well as 229 Republicans.

In a caption students should explain how this situation is like—and unlike—the conflict between the Greeks and the Trojans (one that began with Paris's insult to Menelaos and ended with the deaths of countless soldiers on both sides) and the tension between Akhilleus and Agamémnon (with the former refusing the latter's truce-proposal).

3. Look through newspapers and news magazines for descriptions of recent warfare. Discuss how the battles are similar to those waged between the Greeks and Trojans 3000 years ago. You might also try putting the description into a form like the one Homer might use.

   For example, discuss how this description of atrocities in Bosnia compares with what happened during the battles between Greeks and Trojans:

   2 Serb Chiefs Are Indicted in Massacre

   "Judge Fouad Riad said evidence submitted by chief prosecutor Richard Goldstone depicts 'scenes of unimaginable savagery: thousands of men executed and buried in mass graves, hundreds of men buried alive, men and women mutilated and slaughtered, children killed before their mothers' eyes, a grandfather forced to eat the liver of his own grandson. These are truly scenes from hell, written on the darkest pages of human history,' Riad said..." (*Washington Post,* 11/17/95)

4. Find out about present day tensions between Greece and Turkey. Are these reminiscent of any conflicts in the *Iliad?*